WINNIPEG

MAY 1 0 2011

PUBLIC LIBRARY

WITHDRAWN

Grammar Matters
The Social Significance of How We Use Language

D1018587

Copyright © 2010 Jila Ghomeshi

Arbeiter Ring Publishing
201E-121 Osborne Street
Winnipeg, Manitoba
Canada R3L 1Y4
www.arbeiterring.com

Printed in Canada by Kromar Printing
Cover by Michael Carroll
Second printing, March 2011

Copyright notice

This book is fully protected under the copyright laws of Canada and all other countries of the Copyright Union and is subject to royalty. Any properly footnoted quotation of up to five hundred sequential words may be quoted without permission, so long as the total number of words does not exceed two thousand. For longer continuous quotations or for a greater number of words, contact Arbeiter Ring Publishing for permission.

 MANITOBA ARTS COUNCIL
CONSEIL DES ARTS DU MANITOBA

 Canada Council Conseil des Arts
for the Arts du Canada

Canadian Patrimoine
Heritage canadien

 Manitoba

With assistance of the Manitoba Arts Council/Conseil des Arts du Manitoba.

We acknowledge the support of the Canada Council for our publishing program.

ARP acknowledges the financial support to our publishing activities of the Manitoba Arts Council/Conseil des Arts du Manitoba, Manitoba Culture, Heritage and Tourism, and the Government of Canada through the Canada Book Fund.

Arbeiter Ring Publishing acknowledges the support of the Province of Manitoba through the Book Publishing Tax Credit and the Book Publisher Marketing Assistance Program.

Printed on 100% recycled paper.

LIBRARY AND ARCHIVES CANADA CATALOGUING IN PUBLICATION

Ghomeshi, Jila, 1964-
     Grammar matters : the social significance of how
we use language / Jila Ghomeshi.

(Semaphore series)
Includes bibliographical references.
ISBN 978-1-894037-44-0

     1. English language--Social aspects. 2. English
language--Grammar. 3. English language--Usage.
4. English language--21st century. 5. Sociolinguistics.
I. Title. II. Series: Semaphore series

PE1074.75.G56 2010   306.44   C2010-906622-7

GRAMMAR MATTERS

THE SOCIAL SIGNIFICANCE
OF HOW WE USE LANGUAGE

Jila Ghomeshi

ARBEITER RING PUBLISHING · WINNIPEG

CONTENTS

I

INTRODUCTION

This book is addressed to the people to whom grammar matters. Grammar matters tremendously to many people for many different reasons. People care enough to write letters to the editor of a newspaper or to send e-mail to major media outlets protesting some use of language. Many people believe that grammar ought to be reintroduced as a teaching subject in schools and deplore the state of the language as it is used by youth today. For many of these people, poor grammar is attributable to ignorance, laziness, or lack of education and is therefore justifiably the object of public scorn. For others, grammar is a matter of pride, local identity, or comfort with how things ought to be.

I argue that what people who abhor non-standard grammar are often expressing is a prejudice: a preconceived idea that is not based on reason, experience, or factual knowledge. Expressing a prejudice ought not to make one sound particularly smart since by definition a prejudice is not the result of research and reflection. Yet people who hold prejudices about language often assume they are more intelligent than those who they believe use language incorrectly. While we don't freely express judgments about people based on their race or socio-economic status, we not only feel free to do so on the basis of the way they sound, but feel smug while doing so. In actual fact, neither the use of standard grammar, nor the championing of it, is indicative of superior intelligence. In many cases it is mere intolerance and the articulation of privilege and hierarchy.

There is much talk about language that is not judgmental. Self-proclaimed grammar geeks often offer up facts and trivia about words or race to be the first to identify some new linguistic oddity. People subscribe to "word-of-the-day" newsletters and e-mail lists for the sheer joy of extending their vocabulary. Others look back sentimentally at expressions that have fallen out of circulation, lamenting their loss. In this way we all engage in the construction of an ongoing oral history of our language as it transforms itself. These conversations can be richer and more satisfying once we go beyond classifying anything to do with language as simply good or bad, correct or incorrect. As Stephen Fry writes in a humorous essay[1] on the same themes as this book, it is a shame that we don't share our enjoyment of language in the same way that we speak of music or dance.

As a corollary to the claim that when people judge others for their use of language they are merely articulating their own prejudice, I argue that "errors"—whether misplaced or missing apostrophes, use of slang, politically incorrect terms, or *zee* rather than *zed*—are based on dubious claims to right and wrong. There is no absolute authority to which we can appeal. There are only our own opinions about what we ought to be doing with language and the consensus we reach by sharing them—a consensus that gets constantly renegotiated.

What people who are concerned about language often feel they are defending is clarity, precision, and logic in language. When this concern is expressed in the form of judgment, however, what is created is a widespread insecurity—an insecurity about not speaking well enough—that flares up in many circumstances. Paradoxically, it is this insecurity that contributes to a true lack of coherence, clarity, and communication. The errors made by people who attempt to use a style of language they do not have a command of contribute far more to general meaninglessness in language than the use of a non-standard dialect does. The papers written by first-year university students and Sarah Palin's errors of the *refudiate* kind attest to this problem.

I am, by training, a linguist—the kind who is engaged in the study of the nature of language rather than the kind who speaks many languages. One of my research interests, for instance, is on reduplication: the process by which a word or part of a word is repeated to convey a particular meaning. In Indonesian reduplication of a noun yields a plural meaning: *buku* "book," *buku buku* "books"; in Swahili reduplication of a verb indicates iterativity: *piga* "to strike," *piga piga* "to strike repeatedly." The study of this phenomenon has revealed (a) that there is only a small set of meanings consistently conveyed by reduplication (plural, iterativity, intensity, focus) and (b) that English has a reduplication construction too, one that signals contrastive focus and identifies the prototypical meaning: *Do you want a tuna salad or a salad salad?*[2] This construction goes virtually unnoticed by English speakers themselves yet conforms to an established pattern that we find across languages.

In teaching university students about the properties that span all human languages, then, I talk about recurring patterns and the properties of systems rather than about logic and clarity. In so doing I am continually struck by how what I am teaching runs counter to public opinion on the same matters. My goal here is to begin to reconcile these views so that the stimulating discussions about language that take place in linguistics classes move into public forums as well. If, as is my suspicion, prescriptivism is indicative of an interest in language, there is much to talk about.

To illustrate the point, let's take the popular view that people who say *workin'* instead of *working* are "dropping their g's." The idea that *workin'*, the pronunciation associated with a casual speech style, lacks a [g], while *working*, the standard pronunciation, has one, is mistaken. The "correct" pronunciation of the word *working* does not end in [g]. It ends in a sound that is represented in the International Phonetic Alphabet as [ŋ]. You can hear the difference between [n] and [ŋ] in the middle of the words *sinner* vs. *singer*, and you can hear the difference between [ŋ] alone and [ŋg] in the middle of *singer* vs. *finger*. That the letters "ng" may correspond to [ŋg] as they do in *bingo* (five sounds) or just [ŋ] as they do in *ring* (three sounds) is just one of the many, many inconsistencies of the English spelling system. As for effort, it is practically nonsensical to ask whether [n] takes more or less effort to pronounce at the end of a work than [ŋ]. Is *sin* easier to pronounce than *sing*? And yet our popular description of the difference between *workin'* and *working* as "dropping the 'g'," undoubtedly influenced by written English, incorrectly ascribes less effort to the casual form. What is lacking when someone says *workin'* in the "wrong" context is not a [g] but a good sense of where and when it is appropriate to use this form instead of the standard pronunciation.

Not all opinions about language fall into the categories of prejudice or mistaken beliefs. People have preferences about the way certain words sound, about what sorts of words are appropriate for what settings, and about words that are overused. These preferences can be amusing and newsworthy without being judgmental. For instance, there is a committee at Lake Superior State University that has been soliciting nominees for overused words for over 30 years. The committee publishes its collection of Banished Words (such as "sexting" and "stimulus" in 2010) annually on New Year's Day, which is then widely publicized by the media.[3]

The banished word list is a humorous look at new words that have become annoying through repeated and frequent use. Unfortunately, there are some who do not take these matters light-heartedly. The group of brilliant contributors to Language Log[4] have identified a phenomenon called *word rage*, whereby linguistic preferences are accompanied by expressions of violence towards those who do not conform to them. Clearly this is a psychological rather than grammatical issue.

There is, of course, nothing wrong with having preferences and biases about the forms that language takes if they are recognized as nothing more than that. To use the language of rights, our right to comment on how others use language is as important as our right to choose how we speak in the first place. I wish to defend both and to show that they are not incompatible as long as our opinions don't take the form of judgments that can then have negative social consequences. To these rights I would also like to add a third: we have a right to have access to Standard English, which should be presented as one (of many) varieties of English and as the one that is the most useful in many social circumstances.

Towards the end of this book I'll offer some speculation as to why people feel so strongly about language use and will conclude that opinions and peeves are, for the most part, a natural expression of interest in something that is involved in practically everything we do.

Books aimed at promoting "correct" grammar are often written in an informal, folksy, and humorous way, avoiding the vocabulary of grammar. Words such as "clause," "pronoun," and "tense" are avoided so as to make the work accessible to grammar-phobes, by which I mean people who might be intimidated by the very idea of a grammar book. My goal, however, is to attempt to debunk the idea of a "correct" grammar by addressing grammar *fans*, i.e., people who are comfortable with grammatical terminology and who will relish looking up the terms they have not encountered before. So I will not shy away from using more technical terms and concepts in laying out my argument.

I I

WHAT IS GRAMMAR?

The notion of "grammar" is a complex one as the word is used in numerous different ways by different people. One sense in which linguists use the word is to describe the internalized rules by which people use language. Grammar is the code, the operating system, the means by which we put together sounds, words, and sentences. In this sense *every* speaker uses a grammar regardless of how "well" they speak. Grammar, in this specialized meaning, is essential to mastering a language and to not have grammar would be to have a cognitive impairment—the kind that results from a stroke, for example.

A grammar can also refer to something that is written down. When we study a second language we often consult a grammar—one in which we find verb conjugations, rules on how to ask questions, and so on. A written grammar is an organized summary of a language that probably bears little resemblance to the operating system we use for our native language but one that is nevertheless very useful. This kind of grammar, the written down kind, can take one of two forms. It can either describe or prescribe the way language is used.

Take the following two sentences:

1. *I don't know anything about grammar.*
2. *I don't know nothin' about grammar.*

Despite the clever observation that is often made about two negatives making a positive, the second sentence means exactly the same thing as the first by the people who use it. Both sentences are in wide circulation. The double negative has endured from a time long ago when it was not stigmatized (try googling "double negative Chaucer" to find examples). Moreover, it shows little sign of perishing.

A *descriptive grammar* tells us about the form, meaning, and use of these two sentences. It tells us in what order the words must appear, the position of negation, the appropriate form of the pronoun, and the best choice of preposition. It provides phonetic information (how to pronounce the words) and semantic information (what all the words mean). It describes all aspects of the sentences. A *prescriptive grammar* tells us something else: it tells us which one is better. It tells us that one sentence is correct and the other is incorrect. That one is right and the other is wrong. It tells us not how language *is* used but how language *ought* to be used. Prescriptive grammars involve value judgments.

To say that prescriptive grammars involve evaluative judgments while descriptive grammars do not is not to say that descriptive grammars "condone" socially stigmatized forms of language. There is a difference between describing a double negative and saying it is socially acceptable to go ahead and use it. Descriptive grammars describe forms of language without giving usage advice at all.

While many of us seek to avoid making value judgments about people in general, we see nothing wrong with judging their use of language. Prescriptive grammars reinforce that view. They provide us with an authoritative source on which to base our judgments. Being subject to this sort of judgment can have serious consequences. Using stigmatized forms of language may affect our ability to be accepted in certain social circles, to excel in university, or to obtain the kinds of jobs we want. For this reason it is important to know why some forms of language are more or less acceptable than others. If, as linguists claim, the reasons given by prescriptive grammarians—reasons such as clarity and logic—are not valid, then on what basis can and should we advise others on how to speak? What is at stake in letting go of the idea that some forms of language are better than others? We will see later on that there are ways to maintain language standards without belittling those who flout them. But first let us turn to what it is that actually matters when language judgments are expressed.

III

WHAT IS IT THAT MATTERS?

Language is multi-faceted. It has a written and a spoken form (in the case of signed languages it uses a visual-gestural rather than aural-oral modality). It involves the organization of sounds into words, words into phrases, phrases into sentences, and sentences into narratives. Intonation is to spoken language as punctuation is to written language such that even reading a list of words or providing a telephone number requires a particular kind of intonation. Formulaic exchanges, like greetings, that seem to happen by rote nevertheless involve rules. Linguistic routines such as complimenting others, apologizing, and telling jokes, all have their own formulae. Language is an enormously complex system. We master the rules of our native language effortlessly at a very young age far before many of our other cognitive accomplishments like being able to read, write, or do arithmetic. Our knowledge of the rules of our native language operates below the level of consciousness, freeing up our conscious mind for other activities like reasoning, thinking, and imagining. While we are mostly unaware of what we are doing when *we* use language, we are exquisitely attuned to uses that are different from our own. Variation can be found along every dimension of language use, and inevitably this variation is noted and judged.

In what follows I will sketch out the kinds of things that matter, moving from the smallest units of language (sounds) on to small words (pronouns), bigger words, types of words, dialects, and then whole languages. In doing so I'll survey the various dimensions along which we find differences, disputes, peeves, and proscriptions, from which it will be obvious that there is little, if anything, that is not subject to some sort of ranking and contention. And yet, I will show how untenable are the common assumptions that logic, clarity, or precision distinguish some uses from others.

SOUNDS, PRONUNCIATION, ACCENT

Pronunciation matters. There are many words for which two pronunciations happily coexist and neither is deemed the better one:

3. a) *data* [first syllable rhymes with *bait*, the vowel is a diphthong]

   b) *data* [first syllable rhymes with *bat*, the vowel is a monophthong]

4. a) *often* [the [t] is pronounced]

   b) *often* [the [t] is not pronounced]

5. a) *dew* [rhymes with *new, few*, has an extra [y] sound]

   b) *dew* [rhymes with *do, too*]

In some cases, however, differences in the pronunciation of a word may be a marker of speech style as in the *working/workin'* example. One of the striking points about language that linguists make repeatedly is that the production of sounds in a casual speech style takes no less effort than in a formal speech style, even though the difference is perceived as "sloppy." Similarly, in each of the pairs in (3)-(5) above the (a)-pronunciation contains an extra sound yet no one would make the case that the (b)-pronunciations are "lazier."

In cases where one pronunciation occurs considerably less often than another, competing pronunciation, two possibilities arise: first, that the rarer pronunciation is the prestige one or, second, that the rarer pronunciation is the stigmatized one. An example of the first case is the occurrence of *an historic* instead of *a historic* in speech. This is an unusual pronunciation. Failing to pronounce the [h] at the beginning of *historic*, obscures its relationship to words like *history* in which we do pronounce the [h]. Pronouncing the [h], however, dictates that the preceding article ought to be *a* given the rule that we use *an* before vowels and *a* before consonants. *An historic* has prevailed with an air of formality that gives it high status. As an example of the second case, the pronunciation of *nuclear* as *nucular* has been used by at least three U.S. presidents (Eisenhower, occasionally Clinton, and most famously, George W. Bush[5]). One would think that this ought to be enough to confer status on any term, yet *nucular* remains non-standard, leaving anyone who uses it open to ridicule.

Differences in pronunciation may be indicative of where you live. Small differences in pronunciation based on geography can become big markers of national identity if the pronunciations are on either side of a border. A feature of language that identifies the regional origin of a speaker is called a *shibboleth* and for Canadians there are a number of shibboleths of pronunciation that mark their difference from Americans:[6]

	Canadian pronunciation	**American pronunciation**
last letter of alphabet	*zed*	*zee*
"lieutenant"	*LEFtenant*	*LOOtenant*

These are the pronunciations that people are aware of and can control. For this reason they become the focus of complaints or correction. A distinctively Canadian pronunciation that speakers are *unaware* of producing occurs in words like *mouse* and *out*. The Canadian pronunciation of these words is the one often caricatured by Americans as "moose" and "oot" and goes by the technical name of Canadian Raising. It is unlikely that CBC listeners, for example, will call in outrage if an announcer does *not* have Canadian Raising, and yet it is as much a part of our "accent" as *zed* is.

Within a country, differences in pronunciation can reflect regional dialects or ethnic subgroups. In the U.S., for example, the pronunciation of *ask* as "aks" is a marker of African American speech. A newer trend, also in the U.S., is the use of a glottal stop followed by a full vowel in words like *mountain, button, didn't*. A glottal stop [ʔ] is the gap in the middle of the word *uh oh* "uʔo" so that the word *mountain* sounds like "mounʔin", *button* sounds like "baʔin" and *didn't* sounds like "diʔin". Standard North American pronunciation does not involve a [t] or a [d] in these words either but in the standard version the glottal stop is followed by a reduced syllable. The difference is not a matter of effort—both the new innovation and the standard pronunciation are equal in that respect. Yet, the newer form is judged as sounding "uneducated."

The pronunciation of the consonant "r" seems to be subject to far more than its fair share of value judgments. It is missing in prestige dialects of British English. The presence of "r" in words like *door* and *floor* is considered unrefined. The opposite holds in New York English where the absence of "r" in words like *fourth* and *floor* is the stigmatized pronunciation. The pronunciation of "r" also varies in Canadian French, though neither of the two competing pronunciations sound anything like the English one. There is a trilled "r" and a back-of-the-throat "r'" with the latter being the favoured version in Quebec and the trilled "r" being the stigmatized one.[7]

Finally, differences in pronunciation can be indicative of political outlooks. The pronunciation of Iran and Iraq vary between a first syllable that sounds like *eye* and a first syllable that sounds like *ear*: *eye-ran* vs. *ear-an*. The same difference is found with the first vowel of the word Italian (*eye-talian* vs. *i-talian*). In all three cases the *eye* pronunciation signals greater distance from the country and its people. This distance may be due to unfamiliarity or to hostility. U.S. presidents willing to wage war in the Middle East have tended to use the *eye* pronunciation for Iran and Iraq.

Accent matters. Do you have an accent? You may be aware that you have one if you try to speak another language. Few adult learners of a second language can approximate "native" pronunciation without years of work.

You also may be aware you have one if you speak your native language somewhere else in the world. A Canadian English speaker is often mistaken for an American in Britain—the British not being attuned to the differences in accent between Canada and the U.S. Similarly, the differences between Australian and New Zealand English are imperceptible to most North Americans. But those who live near where they were born and raised are often unaware of their accent. We don't recognize the features of our own accent that provide information about the country and region of our early childhood.

There is no such thing as unaccented English. Britons, Australians, Americans, and Canadians all speak with an accent. Within countries there are regional accents as in a Newfoundland accent or a Southern (U.S.) accent. Accents may evoke certain associations (refinement, class) or judgments about what is "better" (more educated) or "worse" (ignorant). In the case of accents produced by people speaking English as their second (or third or fourth) language, there may be connotations evoked by history (the German accent, the South African accent) or by movies (the French accent and Indian accent of Peter Sellers).

Kids acquire the accents of their peers, not their parents. While this fact is obvious to anyone who has or knows immigrant parents, there are nevertheless misconceptions about whether people with accents interfere with children's abilities to learn "good English." Some such misconception has led the Arizona Department of Education to propose reassigning teachers with "heavy accents" out of classes where students are still learning English.[8] This proposal has been made despite the fact that there is no scientific evidence showing that exposure to accented English delays acquisition and, on the contrary, emerging evidence to suggest that it may help. The negative connotations of having any sort of nonnative accent explains the prevalence of "accent reduction" classes offered on university campuses and at ESL centres and "American accent training" for international call centre employees. There are profits to be made from offering people the chance to learn "unaccented" speech, as absurd as the concept really is.

LETTERS, SPELLING, PUNCTUATION

Spelling matters. Like pronunciation, spelling touches on concerns about patriotism, religion, and politics. For Canadians the choice of *colour* over *color* distinguishes us from Americans and the choice of *organize* over *organise* distinguishes us from the British. For many the use of capital letters for words like *God* vs. *god, Deaf* vs. *deaf,* and *Aboriginal* vs. *aboriginal* is connected to faith, respect, and political identity.

Being able to spell well, especially at a young age, is taken as a sign of intelligence though in actual fact there are brilliant, creative, imaginative people who can't spell well at all. What now spares such people from lifelong stigma and shame is our growing understanding of the various types of dyslexia such as the kind in which people lack the kind of visual memory that constitutes a mental spell checker.

Electronic spell checkers have relieved even non-dyslexic people of the burden of knowing how to spell obscure multi-syllabic words correctly (and being judged accordingly), but have yet to evolve so as to address the problem of homophones—words that have the same pronunciation but different spellings and meanings. Words such as *hegemony, simulacrum,* and *rhizomatic* will get spell-checked but *their/there/they're, its/it's,* and *wear/where* will not be caught if they show up in the wrong place. For this reason, these words are now emblematic of our fears about the decline of spelling.

Punctuation matters. If there was any doubt about the level of public interest in the use and abuse of elements like apostrophes, hyphens, and commas the enormous success of Lynne Truss's book *Eats, Shoots and Leaves* put it to rest. As further evidence of this interest we may note that there is an apostrophe protection society[9] whose *raison d'être* became clearer in early 2009 when the councillors of the city of Birmingham in England voted to ban apostrophes from the city's street signs and much public hand-wringing and despair ensued. The concern about punctuation is almost always focused on what is not being used. Prescriptivists have had little to say, so far, on the new uses for @ and # that we find on Twitter and which make posts virtually incomprehensible to those without a working knowledge of what they mean.

PRONOUNS

Person and number matters. We use pronouns to refer to people[10] who are either present (the speaker and the addressee) or not (people other than speaker/addressee). In English, there are three person distinctions: first person (*I*), second person (*you*), third person (*he/she*), and there are two number distinctions: singular and plural. The three person and two number distinctions yield six categories of pronouns.

First person		Second person	Third person		
singular	plural		singular		plural
		you	fem	masc	*they*
I	*we*		*he*	*she*	

The pronouns we use in English do not correspond neatly to the six categories we have, however. In the second person we have the same form, *you*, used for both singular and plural. In the third person we have two forms, *he/she*, which mark a gender distinction within the singular category but not in the plural. This small matter of a subcategory within a category in the third person has given rise to a great dispute between prescriptive grammarians and the general public.

At issue is this: what if you want to refer to a single individual whose gender you do not know? For instance, what if someone says "I saw the strangest person on the bus today…" and you want to ask about that person? According to prescriptive grammarians, it is not correct to use *they* as in: "Why were they strange?" This is because you are referring to *one* individual and *they* is plural. In the words of one such prescriptivist, Henry W. Fowler, author of *A Dictionary of Modern English Usage*, the use of the plural pronouns *they, them,* and *their* as singulars "sets the literary man's teeth on edge."

In the absence of a third person singular epicene[11] pronoun, prescriptive grammarians have traditionally recommended the use of *he* as a generic over *he or she*, which has been declared "clumsy." Ordinary people, on the other hand, have been quite comfortable using *they*. Consider these examples which all involve third person plural possessive pronoun *their* being used with singular reference:

> **Title of a blog posting:**
>
> Somebody somewhere is eating their hat.

> **From a website on bullying:**
>
> Every recess you join a group of friends who take another student's hat. Everyone laughs when <u>the student</u> runs to get <u>their</u> hat back. What do you?

Moreover, there are contexts in which the use of the masculine-as-generic might be misleading. For instance, if *he/him* is used in the following examples instead of *they/them* there's a very real possibility that the questions could be taken as applying only to men.

> **From a leaflet on the Child Support Agency (UK) website:**
>
> What happens if <u>someone</u> denies <u>they</u> are the parent of a child?

> **A question posed on the Answerbag website:**
>
> If <u>someone</u> had cheated on you, would you get rid of <u>them</u> right away no questions asked?

Uses of the third person plural pronoun as a gender neutral singular have been attested as far back as the 14th century, in the works of renowned writers (Austen, Shakespeare). The proscription against this usage only emerged around the beginning of the 18th century when grammarians started advocating for the use of *he* in sex-indefinite contexts.[12] Their argument was that the use of *they* for a singular antecedent was "inaccurate" in that the number features (plural vs. singular) did not match. Of less concern to them was the fact that there is also a mismatch if *he* is used, namely between masculine and gender-neutral reference.

Third person			
singular			plural
fem	masc	epicene	
she	*he*	*?*	*they*

While it may seem odd to extend the use of a pronoun from plural to singular reference, this is precisely what has happened in the second person. The pronoun *you*, historically plural, came to replace *thou/thee* and has been used for both singular and plural ever since.

Second person	
singular	plural
~~*thou*~~	*you*

One would think that the aversion grammarians have for "inaccuracy" would be somewhat appeased by attempts at the reintroduction of a number distinction in the second person:

Second person	
singular	plural
you	*ya'll* *youse* *you guys* *all y'all*

These forms do not meet with the approval of prescriptivists, however.

NOUNS AND VERBS

Part of speech matters. In English part of speech is fairly fluid and many words can be used as both verbs and nouns: *comb, chart, drive, table,* etc. You can *drink*$_V$ (the *V* indicates verb) *something* or *have a drink*$_N$ (the *N* indicates noun), *book*$_V$ *a holiday* or *read a book*$_N$, *cash*$_V$ *a cheque* or *withdraw some cash*$_N$, etc. Nouns tend to be the largest category of words in any language[13] and often serve as the source for the creation of new verbs (*to google something, to message someone*). There are languages that are even more permissive than English in this respect as well as those that are less permissive in that nouns and verbs rarely overlap. Prescriptivism comes into the picture when a word has had a past life as *only* a noun or a verb. If use of the word extends beyond its traditional word class category then the new use is met with resistance. People decry the use of *impact* and *friend* as verbs and *disconnect* and *reveal* as nouns for no discernable reason other than to protest the change.

Word choice matters. True synonyms are rare in languages. It is quite common, though, to find various ways of saying the same thing that differ in terms of style. The verb *die,* for instance, has casual (*kick the bucket, buy the farm*) and formal (*pass away, expire*) variants. It is considered inappropriate to use too informal a version in a formal context but the casual variants are often more flexible in their range of uses. The relatively recent coining of *bucket list*, referring to a list of things you want to do before you die, could not have been formed with any of its formal counterparts. Contexts of use may be limited in ways other than style. Legal documents are written in "legalese" which contains synonyms for many common words (*buyer ~ purchaser, seller ~ vendor*); academic discourse also involves the proliferation of near synonyms (*history ~ historicism ~ historicity ~ historiography*), the differences among which can signify entire theoretical outlooks. Apparent synonyms may be associated with different communities (*crib ~ home, homey ~ friend, shorty ~ girlfriend*) and in these cases it is hard to separate an outsider's distaste for the choice of word from their opinions about the people who use it.

With certain sets of synonyms, one may be singled out as taboo (*poop ~ shit ~ excrement ~ feces ~ bowel movement*), meaning that the use of that word is prohibited in formal contexts, in the media, on television, etc. There is a great deal of arbitrariness about what we deem to be a taboo word. About the only thing that is *not* arbitrary is the small set of topics that taboo words name across languages and cultures:

Concepts that give rise to taboo language across different cultures
• acts that are inappropriate for "polite company"
• words for sexual intercourse
• words for genitals and sex organs
• words for illegitimate parentage
• words with religious connotations

For each of the concepts that make up the list above, there are one or two expressions naming them that are taboo (*to have intercourse ~ to have sex ~ to make love ~ to fuck*). The arbitrariness about the particular form that is deemed taboo comes from the fact that there's nothing about the string of sounds that makes it intrinsically "filthy" (consider *phoque*, the word for "seal" in French, which the French are quite comfortable with). Nor is there anything about the meaning that is necessarily problematic given that there are non-taboo ways of saying the same thing. Besides, if it were the content of the words wouldn't the words *rape, murder, incest* be taboo? The arbitrariness leads to the peculiar fact that CDs appear with warning labels if they contain "foul language" but not if they contain sexist or violent lyrics. In fact, it isn't really the meaning or content of the words at all that causes offence but the way the words get used. Swearing *at* someone is offensive even if a euphemism is used. The intent behind the words is the offensive part and any word can be made to sound like an insult in the mouth of someone disrespectful. At the other end of the spectrum, people who pride themselves on never swearing may nevertheless do so in a trying situation, even if just to themselves. In this case swearing is driven by our need to vocalize strong emotions.

POLITICALLY CORRECT LANGUAGE

Politics matters. Prescriptivists are often outspoken critics of politically correct language—usually on the grounds that tradition trumps personal offence. What is wrong with the tried and true, they ask rhetorically. What underlies their often sarcastic decrying of politically correct terms is the belief that the new terms are unnecessary and that they make language more complicated. The term "political correctness" and its adjectival counterpart "politically correct" are almost always used pejoratively. When people issue the disclaimer that they are not speaking politically correctly they usually mean they are opting for plain old-fashioned language without any of the new-fangled alternatives proposed only for the purposes of fashion and novelty. More subtly, by positioning themselves as users of "plain" language, they deflect the potential charge that they are using offensive language. A spade is a spade, right?

The spade-is-a-spade view is actually riddled with misunderstandings of how we use language. To start with, the idea that there is only one (plain) name for anything is false. From the moment we start acquiring language we learn that there is more than one name for the same person, place, or thing. A child learns that her mother (*mummy ~ mom ~ mama*) has a given name that people call her. Depending on the language, she may learn that there are different terms for her mother's sister and her father's sister (both *aunt* in English). While sorting out kinship terms, she will also be learning to respond to numerous names herself (*darling ~ sweetie ~ honey ~ puppy ~ boodles*). She has to start sorting out which names belong with which objects (a *kitty cat ~ kitten ~ cat* is different from a *puppy ~ doggie ~ dog* but both can be a *pet* or *animal*). She will learn many quirks of the language such as the fact that cars, trucks, and motorcycles have *drivers* but planes have *pilots* and ships have *captains*.

Names may vary in terms of style (formal, informal) and intimacy (used between friends or strangers) but they also vary over time as they take on new connotations or lose old ones. The term *politically correct* illustrates precisely this point.[14] At its inception in the 70s, the term was used without irony by Maoists to describe positions that should be taken (by Maoists) on political issues like Black Nationalism, for example. But it soon became more generally used by those on the social democratic left to poke fun at those (Maoists/Stalinists) whose politics seemed too rigid. In its ironic usage, being "PC" meant being too dictatorial and was often used in a self-mocking way by those on the left. By the late 70s it had come to refer not just to political positions but also to language. At some point soon after that the term was adopted by those on the right in a pejorative way. It shifted from being a term that people use to be ironic about themselves to being a term people use to unfavourably describe others. This shift moves in the opposite direction of the one that takes place when a term is reclaimed. In the case of a word like *queer* for lesbian or gay people, it is used by the people to whom it has been unfavourably applied as an ironic label for themselves.[15]

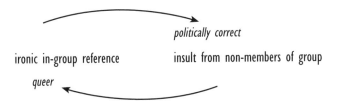

politically correct

ironic in-group reference   insult from non-members of group

queer

There are domains in which terminology has undergone revision and change simply because of unfavourable connotations. Adoptive parents, for instance, are often given linguistic recommendations about using *birth mother* over *real mother* and *biological child* instead of *child of one's own*. Adoption professionals are counselled to use the term *relinquished* over *abandoned*. The lack of public complaint about these sorts of changes suggests that there is more than simply a defence of traditional terms when political correctness is invoked.

Let's consider the most widespread change in English that is considered to have been spearheaded by forces of "political correctness": the substitution of gender-neutral terms for gendered ones. The motivation on the part of those who have advocated for this change has been that gender should be irrelevant when it comes to one's marital status or profession. Thus we have seen shifts like the following:

6. a) *Mrs. vs. Miss* ⇨ *Ms.*
    b) *stewardess* ⇨ *flight attendant*
    c) *waiter vs. waitress* ⇨ *server*
    d) *fireman* ⇨ *firefighter*
    e) *postman* ⇨ *letter carrier*
    f) *chairman* ⇨ *chair*

There have also been shifts in the names we use to refer to minority groups:

7. a) *negro* ⇨ *coloured* ⇨ *black* ⇨ *African American*
    b) *Indian* ⇨ *American Indian* ⇨ *aboriginal* ⇨ *native American* ⇨ *First Nations*
    c) *crippled* ⇨ *disabled* ⇨ *differently abled* ⇨ *person with disabilities*
    d) *retarded* ⇨ *mentally challenged* ⇨ *developmentally delayed*

The names for white, able-bodied people have not changed at the same pace. In fact, it is hard to identify the appropriate labels. The term *neurotypical* is a relatively recent coining by those in the autistic community for people who are not on the autism spectrum and the term *breeders* is sometimes applied to heterosexuals with children. In general, though, what is considered "normal" goes unnamed so that we have *bald* but not *haired*, *one-armed* but not *two-armed*, etc. The name for the phenomenon by which the "normal" goes unnamed is *exnomination*[16] or *default (sub)category erasure*.[17]

Returning to the changes we've seen with regard to the names for minority groups, the point is that these are not contentious because they are *changes*. There are many other changes that do not receive the same amount of (negative) attention. Consider the new labels for low-prestige jobs, the coining of which is presumably motivated by the desire to elevate the status of the work, cast off negative connotations, and/or to reflect changes in the way the work is carried out:

8. a) *secretary* ⇨ *administrative assistant*
   b) *prison guard* ⇨ *corrections officer*
   c) *clerk* ⇨ *sales associate*
   d) *hair dresser* ⇨ *hair stylist* ⇨ *hair associate*

   e) *person who works at* Subway *(sandwich place)*
     ⇨ *sandwich artist*
   f) *prostitute* ⇨ *sex worker/sex trade worker*
   g) *mortician* ⇨ *funeral director*

These changes are less likely to be perceived as "politicizing" the language than the move toward gender-neutral labels has been. What is revealed is that the degree to which a change of name makes us uncomfortable reflects our attitudes and feelings towards the group it names. This is a particular instance of the main argument in this book: that many discussions of language substitute objectionable judgments that we would not make about people with seemingly more acceptable claims focused on language.

The politicizing of language brings into conflict a number of beliefs we operate by: that people have the right to choose their own names; that people have a right to use language as they wish; and that people have a right to comment on others' use of language. It is the right of people to choose their own names that comes under attack when we make fun of "political correctness," yet the intensity of the scorn we have for name changes is inversely proportional to the power of the group wishing to be renamed.

The politics of word choice does not always involve change. What may be contested is to whom the word may be correctly applied. What is the difference between a *geek*, a *dork*, and a *nerd*? Can Sarah Palin be considered a *feminist* if she calls herself one?[18] The debates around definitions of words extend beyond categories of people. Is the civil union between two people of the same sex a *marriage*? Can the word *apartheid* be applied to Israel?[19]

Ultimately, whether a proposed change is viewed as "political" depends also on who is proposing it. When 18th-century grammarians began advocating for the use of *he* in sex-indefinite contexts there was no documented outcry. When 1970s feminists proposed that *he* should not be used when the referent includes women, their "demands" were viewed as an attempt to alter the English language.

DIALECTS

Dialect matters. When speakers of the same language have different accents and some differences in vocabulary and grammar then we say they are speaking different dialects. For example, in addition to the difference in accent between British English and American English, we find accompanying differences in vocabulary (*trunk ~ boot, truck ~ lorry, diapers ~ nappies*) as well as in constructions like *have you any wool?* (British) and *I'm gonna buy me a car* (American South). Speakers of different dialects can still understand each other. If speakers can't understand each other then we say they are speaking different languages. This difference between a dialect and a language is called mutual intelligibility. As it turns out, there are dialects that are *not* mutually intelligible within a country (e.g., Germany) and languages that *are* mutually intelligible across national borders (dialects of Spanish and Portuguese, Swedish, and Norwegian). In this way politics intersects with the diagnostic of mutual intelligibility and the difference between dialect and language is more aptly summed up by the aphorism "a language is a dialect with an army and a navy."[20]

When different dialects coexist within the same geographic region it is rare that they are recognized as different but equal. Usually the variety that is closer to the standard (the one used in the media and taught in schools) is considered the proper one while the other may not be recognized as a dialect at all but as an amusing approximation of the standard (as in the perception of the Newfoundland dialect in Canada or of Appalachian English in America). In some cases, the non-standard variety is viewed as just plain incorrect. In California, for example, this issue of dialect vs. degraded speech was at the heart of the controversy that erupted over the recognition of Ebonics, also known as African American Vernacular English (AAVE).

In December 1996, the School Board of Oakland, California, proposed to "recognize" Ebonics in order to better teach speakers of it to read and write Standard English. By treating students as speaking a different variety of

English rather than as speaking a degraded form out of laziness, the Oakland School Board believed that the teachers they represented would have greater success in teaching the standard. The storm of protest that followed was based, in part, on the mistaken belief that the authorities intended to teach Ebonics *instead* of Standard English. The Linguistic Society of America, among other institutions, addressed the controversy with a statement that concluded as follows:

> *There is evidence from Sweden, the US, and other countries that speakers of other varieties can be aided in their learning of the standard variety by pedagogical approaches which recognize the legitimacy of the other varieties of a language. From this perspective, the Oakland School Board's decision to recognize the vernacular of African American students in teaching them Standard English is linguistically and pedagogically sound.*[21]

LANGUAGES

Language matters. While we often hear about the inferiority of one dialect in comparison with another (usually because it is not the standard one), it is much more rare to hear the same position taken with respect to two different languages. And yet the belief that most languages are equal to each other does not prevent the imposition of one over the other in numerous political contexts.

There are cases where one language is deemed the only official one for the purposes of uniting people or silencing dissent. For instance, Russian was imposed on speakers of "ethnic" languages in the former Soviet Union. The original motive may have been to create a *lingua franca* (common language) but the motive was soon reinterpreted as one of creating a monolingual Russian state. Part of regaining independence has been a reassertion of language rights and policies favouring local languages over Russian. Similarly, in Spain under Franco in the mid-20th century the use of Catalan was banned in government-run institutions and at public events.

A language may be imposed on speakers of other languages as part of an attempt to assimilate them. In Canada from the 19th century onwards, English was insisted upon in the residential schools which aboriginal children were forced attend as part of a broader assimilation campaign. Students were punished for speaking their first language and the subsequent loss of those languages was emblematic of a more general loss of culture and identity that proved devastating for this population.

One language may be legislated as the public one in order to protect minority rights. In French-speaking Quebec, controversial sign laws dictate that French must predominate on outdoor commercial signs. The motivation is to protect French, a minority language within Canada, from the encroachment of English.

One language may be legislated as the public one for fear that it may *become* a minority language. This appears to be the motivation behind English-only movements in the U.S. For instance, in January 2009 the people of Nashville, Tennessee, were sent to the polls to vote on a bill that would forbid city officials to conduct business in any language other than English.[22] Voters overwhelmingly defeated the bill. Other motivations include "cost-saving." This was the reason given by Republican Alabama gubernatorial candidate Tim James who vowed in a campaign in spring 2010 that, if elected, he'd give the state driver's licence exam only in English.

The point of this somewhat superficial survey of what matters in language has been twofold. In addition to showing the range of phenomena about which we have strong opinions, I have also tried to expose places where the concern is a cover for other issues—issues such as discomfort with minority groups, suspicion of those who don't sound like us, and the idea that multilingualism can be threatening to culture and tradition. I will now turn to another part of the picture, namely the problem with the most common reasons given to justify these attitudes.

IV

THE FALLACIES OF PRESCRIPTIVISM

IV-I THE FALLACY OF LOGIC

One of the reasons that people often give for judging some form of language as undesirable is that it is not logical. For example, those who are bothered by the expression *I could care less* point out that it is used to mean *I don't care*. Logic tells us that if one doesn't care, it shouldn't be possible to care less. Logically then, the expression ought to be *I couldn't care less*, but in the real world people use both *I couldn't care less* and *I could care less* to mean the same thing.

Condemning a form of language for not being logical presumes, of course, that language *is* logical. If we turn to the study of logic, however, we learn that natural language is utterly inadequate for the purpose of representing logical notions. For this reason, the first thing that is taught in a logic class is a special language. Even with its special language, logic can easily get contaminated by the messy meanings and imprecision that the corresponding English words carry.

Take, for instance, the word *and*. The logical symbol for *and*, ∧, is meant to simply connect two conjuncts in any order. Thus, in logic the following two sentences are supposed to mean the same thing:

9. a) *I fell down the stairs and I broke my arm.*
    b) *I broke my arm and I fell down the stairs.*

For English speakers, however, these two sentences are not paraphrases. The first implies that falling down the stairs happened first and was the cause of breaking my arm while the second implies that my breaking my arm happened first and was the cause of my falling down the stairs. In other words, the English word *and* has temporal and causal connotations that the logical symbol does not have. It is precisely because of these connotations that the full range of meanings of the English word *and* can't be modelled by logic.

Internal to a given language there are numerous irregularities that contribute to an overall lack of logic. Consider the reflexive pronouns in English. Reflexive pronouns are pronouns that end in *-self.* One of the ways they are used is to indicate that an action is performed on and by the same individual (the subscripted numbers 1, 2, 3 indicate first, second, and third person respectively):

10. a) I_1 *saw John*$_3$.
    b) I_1 *saw you*$_2$.
    c) I_1 *saw ~~I, me~~, myself*$_1$.

There are three forms of each pronoun in English—one that appears in subject position (nominative), one that appears in object position (accusative), and one that appears as a possessor (genitive).[23] Reflexive pronouns combine the word *-self* with genitive pronouns in the first and second person but with accusative pronouns in the third person. There is no logical reason for this.

	First person		**Second person**	**Third person**		
	singular	**plural**		**singular**		**plural**
				fem	masc	
nominative	*I*	*we*	*you*	*she*	*he*	*they*
accusative	*me*	*us*		*her*	*him*	*them*
genitive	*my*	*our*	*your*		*his*	*their*
reflexive	*myself*	*ourselves*	*yourself/selves*	*herself*	*himself*	*themselves*

Turning to verbs, we find another area where logic is sacrificed so as to maintain tradition. The regular way to form the past tense (also known as the preterite) in English is to add the suffix *-ed* to the base form of verbs. This pattern is deemed "regular" because it is the one applied to new verbs (*friend – friended*), the one elicited in experiments involving made-up verbs, and the pattern that is over-applied by children when they are acquiring English (e.g., *do–doed, go–goed, catch–catched* are all commonly heard in the speech of 3–4 year-olds). We also have a small group of verbs for which the past tense is formed in "irregular" ways (*teach–taught, sing–sang, do–did, go–went*). The fact that the irregular group is comprised of our most frequently used verbs attests to the fact that there is strong pressure to regularize. Only the most frequent verbs resist this pressure and maintain their irregularities; but there is nothing that would be lost in terms of meaning if *all* verbs took *-ed*.

Likewise, there is no logical reason why some verbs distinguish the preterite from the part participle (*I drove – I have driven*). We suffer no loss or ambiguity of meaning with the (large) class of verbs that don't exhibit this distinction (*I walked – I have walked, I love – I have loved, I clean – I have cleaned*, etc.). If we decided tomorrow that all verbs should take *-ed* in the past tense and use the same form for the past participle, we could function as well as we do now. What we'd lose wouldn't be logic but tradition and history. The almost visceral sense of discomfort Standard English speakers feel when they hear *I seen it* is about the loss of a distinction (*saw–seen*). It is not about loss of clarity, precision and logic given that the majority of our verbs don't exhibit this distinction in the first place.

To reinforce the idea that puzzles abound in English and also for the fun of it, let's consider the following examples.

Fact: In English, particles like *up, out,* and *off* can be used before or after a direct object, but if the direct object is a pronoun, the particle has to follow it.

11. a) *pick the baby up ~ pick up the baby*
    b) *throw garbage out ~ throw out garbage*
    c) *take clothes off ~ take off clothes*
    a) *pick her up ~ ??? pick up her*
    b) *throw it out ~ ??? throw out it*
    c) *take them off ~ ??? take off them*

Fact: The direct object and indirect object of a Germanic verb like *give* can be switched around so that there are two possible ways of saying the same thing, but the Latinate equivalent, *donate*, doesn't have two corresponding word orders.

12. a) *give an apple to the teacher ~ give the teacher an apple*
    b) *donate a painting to the museum ~ ??? donate the museum a painting*

Fact: In English expressions like *the hell, the heck, on earth, the fuck* can be inserted right after a clause-initial question word like *what, who, how*, and *which*. But not in all cases for reasons that are not obvious.

13. a) *What the heck did you see?*
      ?? What the heck number did you dial?
    b) *Who on earth left their shoes here?*
      ?? Which on earth candidate would run a negative campaign?
    c) *How the hell did he pass the course?*
      ?? How the hell many windows have you broken?

In each of the cases above there is no explanation based on logic that can explain the facts. Explanations have to do with the historical development of syntactic patterns.

The notion of logic is equally nonsensical when we start looking across languages, not simply within them. In English nouns do not have gender, in French they have two (masculine, feminine) and in German they have three (masculine, feminine, neuter). There is no logical reason for this. In Blackfoot all kinship terms (*mother, daughter, uncle*) must appear with a possessor (e.g., *my, your, his*). There is no logical reason for this. In English, there is a gender distinction in the third person singular pronouns (*he, she*) while in Persian there is just one gender-neutral third person singular pronoun (*u*). Quite apart from the fact that there is no logical reason for this, there is clearly no connection between this aspect of language and society. Iran, where Persian is spoken, is clearly not a more gender-neutral society than the countries in which English is spoken.

Perhaps the best example of a system that we use and which is completely lacking in logic is our writing system. Writing comes after speech in development of an individual human. Children are well on their way to speaking at age two but don't start learning to write till at least four or five. While the acquisition of word order, for instance, seems to happen effortlessly, the idea of reading and writing from left to right is something that has to be explicitly taught. Writing also comes much later than speech in the evolution of the species. The earliest cave drawings are estimated to have been made around 15,000 B.C.E., while language is thought to have first appeared anywhere between 30,000 to 100,000 years ago.

The English writing system is alphabetic (from Greek *alpha, beta, the* first two letters of the Greek alphabet), meaning that each symbol is meant to represent one sound. There are also writing systems that are consonantal, meaning that only the consonants and not the vowels are represented. Such systems are used for Semitic languages such as Hebrew and Arabic. Syllabic writing systems where a symbol corresponds to a syllable are used for Japanese, Cherokee and Cree. Logographic systems where a symbol corresponds to roughly a word are used for Chinese languages.

A number of different languages can share a writing system, as is the case with Chinese languages. It is also the case that the same language may have been represented by different writing systems over time. In Azerbaijan, Turkmenistan, and Uzbekistan, for instance, where Turkic languages are spoken, the Arabic alphabet was used prior to 1940. Early Soviets imposed the Roman alphabet in the 1920s, which in turn was replaced by the Cyrillic alphabet in 1940 under Stalin and Soviet domination. In the early 1990s the three former provinces of the Soviet Union announced that they were returning to the use of the Roman alphabet.

Returning to English and the one-symbol-for-one-sound alphabetic writing system that we supposedly use, even the most cursory consideration reveals that the reality is far more complicated, messy, and illogical than the intended goal. Let's start with the fact that there are around 40 sounds in English but only 26 letters. Obviously that means more than one sound may correspond to a single letter (first and second *c* in *circle*). But, confusingly, a single sound can also correspond to a number of different letter combinations. All of the following words start with the same sound: *psychology, sense, cent* and all of the following words end with the same sound: *back, look, cheque.* The word *judge* begins and ends with the same sound but not the same letters. Silent letters abound like *e*'s at the ends of words and the *gh* in *through* and *thought* but not in *laugh*. You can't always look at a word and know how to pronounce it and you can't always hear a word and know how to spell it. Mastering English spelling is a spectacular feat of memorization.

One of the people most irked by the English spelling system was the famous Irish playwright and author George Bernard Shaw (recipient of both a Nobel Prize for literature and an Oscar for the screenplay for *Pygmalion*). He was an outspoken advocate for spelling reform and committed enough to the cause to leave money for it in his will. His well-known example to illustrate the absurdity of our writing system is the word *ghoti* which he claimed could be a possible spelling for the word "fish" if we use the *gh* at the end of *rough*, the *o* in the first syllable of *women* and the *ti* in the word *nation*.

The messiness and chaos of English spelling is attributable to a number of factors. First, no writing system keeps up with sound change and English is no exception. Contemporary spelling reflects older pronunciations. The current spelling of most English words is based on Late Middle English (11th century up to 1470) or early Modern English (latter half of 15th century to 1650) pronunciations. In other words, our spelling reflects the pronunciation of Chaucer and Shakespeare's time. Moreover, this spelling system wasn't *ever* regular and systematic. When the printing press was introduced, printers often misspelled words and archaic and idiosyncratic spellings were common.[24] And when the need for spelling reform was recognized in the Renaissance (1450–1600), spellings were changed not to reflect the pronunciation of words but to conform to their etymologies. Thus, Middle English *dette* was "reformed" to *debt* though the pronunciation never involved a [b].

English spelling demonstrates the adherence to a system (writing) that is slower to change than the system it represents (sounds). In fact, we adhere to systems even if the motivation for their original design no longer holds. Take the QWERTY keyboard, as a non-linguistic example. The layout was designed in order to avoid jams on the early "writing machines," i.e., typewriters. A jam could be caused by two neighbouring typebars being hit at the same time. The solution was to arrange commonly used letter-pairs like "th" and "st" so that their typebars were not side-by-side. We no longer use typewriters with typebars that hit a piece of paper. There is nothing that can jam when we type at great speed. And yet we stick with the QWERTY keyboard because that is what we are used to.

I don't mean to downplay the reasons we are slow to change or to suggest that these reasons are trivial. But if we talk about what they are—maintenance of custom, tradition, and comfort—we see that "logic" is not one of them.

I V - I I   THE FALLACY OF PRECISION

Setting: a large park where two families with small children are picnicking. A three-and-a-half-year-old, noticing the big stick that her age-mate from the other family is playing with, complains to her mother that she wants one too. Her mother gestures to a big tree nearby and says, "Go and look under that tree." The girl returns a few moments later to announce, with frustration, that "the tree is too heavy for me to lift."

English is not precise. No natural (as opposed to artificial) language is precise, which makes the accomplishment of children all the more remarkable. One contributing factor to this lack of precision is polysemy, as exhibited by the word *under* in the example above. Polysemy refers to a case where a word has different but related meanings.[25] An adult, for example, might know that *under a tree* actually means the area of ground under its branches, while a child might interpret *under a tree* as meaning underneath the entire object, including its roots. Polysemy abounds in natural language. There is recent research by cognitive linguists that concentrates, for example, on the polysemy exhibited by common everyday prepositions like *over, under, in*, etc. Let's take *over* as an illustrative example.[26] In the sentence in (14a) below, *over* expresses a static spatial relationship between two objects, while in (14b) the relationship is dynamic.

14. a) *The lamp hangs **over** the table.*

b) *The plane flew **over** the city.*

In (15a) the dynamic relationship involves a curved-arc path, while in (15b) the movement is simply on an axis.

15. a) *He jumped **over** the wall.*

b) *He turned **over** the stone.*

In (16a) there is a covering relationship expressed between two objects with one on top of the other while in (16b) the covering relationship does not involve a vertical dimension.

16. a) *He laid the tablecloth **over** the table.*

b) *He put his hands **over** his face.*

In (17a) and (17b) metaphorized uses of *over* conceptualize power in terms of vertical space and an event in terms of an obstacle.

17. a) *He has no authority **over** me.*

b) *He got **over** his parents' deaths.*

These examples are but a small subset of the meanings *over* can express and they illustrate the way in which a single preposition can have a range or network of meanings. For this reason, it is hard to determine what the "core" or precise meaning of any given preposition is, and indeed whether there is such a thing is a matter of debate among linguists. The lack of one basic meaning may explain the kind of arbitrariness around the use of prepositions which makes them so hard to learn in a second language. Consider, for instance, the use of *in* and *on* in (18):

18. a) *She put the apple* **in** *the bag.*
    b) *She put the apple* **on** *the bag.*

In this case the choice of *in* suggests enclosure by another object while *on* does not. But in the following examples this distinction in meaning appears to be reversed:

19. a) *She lives* **in** *Canada.*
    b) *She got* **on** *the bus.*

Among the factors that give rise to widespread polysemy across languages is the pervasiveness of metaphor. Beyond its use as a poetic or literary device, metaphor is rife in our common everyday language. Metaphor refers to the use of one concept to understand and talk about another, unrelated, concept. It is often contrasted with "literal" language but as researchers on metaphor, notably George Lakoff, have shown, the line between metaphoric and literal language is hard to locate. The ubiquity of metaphor is what makes endeavours like machine translation, which depend on a fixed meaning for every word, virtually impossible.

Consider, for instance, the way in which we transfer the vertical spatial orientation (up vs. down) onto abstract domains like feelings, health, values, and morals:[27]

HAPPY IS UP
I'm feeling *up*.
My spirits *rose*.

You're in *high* spirits these days.

SAD IS DOWN
I'm feeling *down*.
He's really *low* these days.
I'm *depressed*.
My spirits *sank*.

HEALTH AND LIFE ARE UP

He's at the *peak* of health
He's in *top* shape.
His health is *declining*.

SICKNESS AND DEATH ARE DOWN
He *fell* ill.
He came *down* with the flu.

GOOD IS UP
Things are looking *up*.

He does *high*-quality work.
We hit a *peak* last year, but it's been *downhill* ever since.

BAD IS DOWN
Things are all an all-time *low*.
He *fell* from power.

VIRTUE IS UP
He is *high*-minded.
She has *high* standards.
She is an *upstanding* citizen.
That was a *low-down* thing to do.

DEPRAVITY IS DOWN
That was a *low* trick.
Don't be *underhanded*.
I wouldn't *stoop* to that.

Given that metaphors map one domain of experience onto another, we might ask where the starting point is. Researchers in this field claim that the "basic" or non-metaphoric concepts are not "literal" but rather concepts that are grounded in our physical experience. For example, given that a range of our own physiological states are understood in terms of heat, temperature serves as a rich source of metaphors for describing others (e.g., *she's hot, she's warm, she's cool, she's cold*).

While our physical experiences may serve as the source for much of our metaphoric language, this is not to say that our words for them are precise. In fact, bodily sensations are often the most difficult things to describe in words. My daughter, at the age of three, often puzzled me by crying out uncomfortably *my foot is making noise.* I eventually figured out what she meant and offered her the "correct" versions (*you have pins and needles* or *your foot has fallen asleep*), neither of which was really any more precise than her own description.

Precision, like many other concepts, can only be assessed in terms of how accurately a message has been conveyed, not in terms of the form the message has taken. When someone declares another person's language to be unclear and imprecise what is implicit is that it is unclear and imprecise *to them.* Such statements obscure the shared responsibility we have for achieving understanding.

If we move away from the meanings of individual words we find other factors at play that give rise to imprecision and ambiguity. We use a lot of shorthand in communicating with one another and one of our shorthand devices is metonymy, something closely related to metaphor but distinct from it. Metonymy refers to the use of one word to refer to something associated with it. Metonymy and metaphor both involve the use of a word or concept to stand in for another, but with metonymy the two concepts are associated in some way while with metaphor they are completely unrelated. The following examples illustrate different types of metonymy:

20. a) *the kettle is boiling* (container for contents)
    b) *Dickens is on the top shelf* (name of author for his/her work)
    c) *we need some new faces around here* (part for whole)
    d) *daisy dukes* (name of famous wearer for item worn, in this case shorts)
    e) *9/11* (date an event occurred to refer to the event)

In (20c) we have the use of a part for a whole but we can also use the whole for a part. Consider the way in which we use *the car* to stand in for different parts in the following:[28]

21. a) *wash the car* (usually means the outside of it)
    b) *vacuum the car* (usually means the inside of it)

    c) *fill up the car* (usually means the gas tank)
    d) *service the car* (usually means its brakes,
       engine, etc.)

Cognitive linguists have observed that to be more precise in the case of examples like (21) would yield excruciatingly wordy and long utterances. We use metonymy because it provides us with a kind of shorthand.

Shorthand is not a spontaneous time-saving device but is actually built in to the grammar of languages. Pronouns, for example, provide a shorthand way of referring to people already introduced. We opt for pronouns to avoid repeating names and identifying descriptions:

22. a) *Mary walked into the room.* **She** *took off her coat.*
    b) *The man in the yellow hat walked into the room.*
      He *took off his coat.*

Given that shorthand begets ambiguity, however, we can find lots of cases where there is more than one possible referent (person referred to) for a pronoun:

23. a) *John thinks that Mary is happy with* **his** *decision.*
      his = John's
    b) *John thinks that Bill is happy with* **his** *decision.*
      his = John's or Bill's

24. a) *John told Mary that* **he** *should be finished work by 6:00.*
      he = John

b) *John told Bill that* **he** *should be finished work by 6:00.*

   he = John or Bill

To be anti-ambiguity in these cases is to be anti-pronoun. There is simply no way to be more precise apart from repeating the name of the intended referent. Most people opt for ambiguity on the grounds that the pronouns sound much more natural in sentences like these. There is no such thing as ambiguity-free language.

So far we've been looking at the imprecision of words and the sentences in which they appear. We could call this structural imprecision—imprecision that arises from the structure of the language. But quite apart from this kind of imprecision there is also deliberate imprecision used by speakers in the service of linguistic politeness. Linguistically, being polite is often expressed through being indirect in some way or another.

Using pronouns to illustrate once more, we know that prescriptive grammarians frown upon the use of plural *they* for a singular referent in English. In many languages, however, using the second person plural pronoun for a singular referent is a way of being polite. In French, for instance, the second person plural *vous* is used instead of its singular counterpart *tu* in order to express formality and respect toward someone older or in some way socially superior.

Second person	
Singular	plural
tu	*vous*

In some languages the same strategy is used in the first person as well. In English, choice of *we* over *I* is no longer necessary to signal politeness although it is still used in some genres of scientific and academic writing for formality. Using the first person plural to refer to oneself outside of those genres is sometimes called the "royal *we*." To address a royal person, we find super-polite forms that dispense with the second person altogether and use third person as a form of address (*Would her highness like more tea?*). And in some languages (e.g., Persian), *third* person plural pronouns are used to address an esteemed individual (*Would they like some tea?*).

	First person		Second person	Third person		
	singular	plural		singular		plural
Nominative	*I*	*we*	*you*	fem	masc	*they*
				she	*he*	

A newer form of politeness has emerged in English whereby reflexives are used in place of simple pronouns. This strategy is particularly evident in service-industry-speak (waiters in restaurants asking *and for yourself?*, business memos ending with *please feel free to contact myself with any further questions*)

Some languages employ a much richer system of pronouns that include both "deferential" and "humiliative" forms but even with these more elaborate systems, the most polite thing to do might be to avoid pronouns altogether. In English we see a little of this in that there are people we only refer to by title (*Mr. Speaker, Mr. President*), and there are families that have a "don't call your mother *she*" rule. But in a language like Urdu, for example, the respectful way of inviting someone to your house is to say something like *Please bring your ennobling presence to the hut of this dustlike person sometime.* In Persian, the most deferential way of referring to oneself is to replace *ma* "we" with *bande* "slave."

While the second person pronoun, *you*, is often considered too direct to be polite when referring to an addressee, it is gradually taking on a new life as a *first* person pronoun. This probably arises out of its use as a generic pronoun, instead of *one*. A generic pronoun is used when one wants to make statements about people in general. Since the use of *one* is declining and it now sounds too fancy for ordinary conversations, *you* is used instead. In other words, you don't use one anymore when speaking casually. Making a personal statement into a generic one is a way of generalizing it beyond one's own experience. If instead of saying *my heart soars when I see migrating geese* you say *your heart soars when you see migrating geese,* you are claiming that anyone would feel the same way.

The use of *you* to mean *I* occurs when people appear to be speaking generically but are describing situations that only they have experienced or participated in. *You-as-I* is most obvious in the speech of celebrities whose lives are hardly of a generic kind. In celebrity-speak an athlete who has just scored a winning goal in an important game or an artist who has just won a lifetime achievement award will talk about how *you* feel in those circumstances. Consider the following excerpt from an interview in which the interviewee switches from *I* to *you* halfway through his answer in talking about a talent that few possess:[29]

TB: *Can you give us your view of the relationship between the muscles in your hands, the mental knowledge you have of the tune, and your artistic expressions when you are playing?*

HA: I really don't think of the muscles in my hand at all. That fortunately takes care of itself. I either play enough or practice enough that there's no problems there. When I'm playing tunes that I'm very familiar with, that I've been playing for years, I don't have to think too much consciously, mentally of either what chord is coming next or what notes I'm going to pick out to play over that. The harmony and the melody are so ingrained that I can basically just try to create motifs and ideas and phrases over the chord changes or over the melody. When I'm playing a tune I'm not quite as familiar with I have to fall back on intellectual devices like I'll try this particular chord superimposed over this one here.

It's a combination of all the above. Ideally, when you're playing your best, you're not really thinking about much of anything and the ideas are just hopefully kind of flowing effortlessly and there's no technical barriers to what you're playing. Occasionally there is. You're trying to play an idea or a phrase and you get hung up somewhere physically or mentally. You'll have to stop and regroup and try something else. But basically it's just a matter of exploring the ideas and trying different things. Sometimes you get some pleasant surprises and sometimes not.

The fact that we find this use of *you* in the speech of celebrities may be because they are so often called upon to talk about themselves at length. In fact, even for the non-famous, there is a notion that direct reference is "vulgar," or that speech containing too much "I/me" is boastful or self-absorbed. We may choose second person over first to "depersonalize" what we are saying or to invite others to imagine themselves as us. Of note is the fact that these considerations weigh as heavily as "precision" in choice of pronoun.

The link between indirectness and politeness also shows up in the use of past tense in service-industry-speak and in encounters between strangers. The past tense is supposed to be used for events that have taken place prior to the moment of speech. However, in-store sales staff will approach browsing customers by asking them "*was there anything you were looking for?*" and a person in a crowded elevator might ask someone who has just entered "*what floor did you need?*" The use of the past tense in these cases is technically imprecise and certainly illogical but is nevertheless considered polite. To insist on precision would rob language of the nuances that we ultimately associate with being "civilized."

Quite apart from factors such as polysemy, metaphor, metonymy, and politeness, imprecision may arise simply from the use of conventional turns of phrase. It is quite common for the hosts of regular radio programs to say *see you tomorrow* or *see you next week*. While technically imprecise, their meaning is perfectly clear. It is also quite common to hear the statement *your call is important to us* as you experience wait times on the phone which demonstrate the opposite. The statement ceases to have any meaning, let alone one that is imprecise.

IV - III   THE FALLACY OF AUTHORITY

There are a great many people who firmly believe in proper grammar, correct language, and following the right rules. Many of the same people are unable to identify where the rules of grammar come from. We have seen that logic and precision are not guiding principles when it comes to the organization of language but there are nevertheless rules at work suggesting that there is some authority to which we can appeal. Who makes these rules up?

It turns out that there are few languages that have committees or legislative bodies responsible for determining what is proper and correct. There is a French Academy (l'Académie française) for all matters pertaining to the use, vocabulary, and grammar of the French language and there are a number of other academies (Swedish, Brazilian, Russian) modeled on the French one, but most languages don't have such an academy, including English.

There are, of course, prescriptive grammars available for consultation. Given their apparent need-fulfilling function, it may come as a surprise that they are a very recent phenomenon in the evolution of language. Dating the beginning of language with any sort of precision has proven virtually impossible. Estimates vary wildly. Let's say we've had language for at least 30,000 years, a conservative estimate.[30] Prescriptive grammars have been in existence for only about 300 of those 30,000 years. Not only did we lack prescriptive grammars before the 18th century, we didn't even have a means to write them for the first 20,000 years—writing systems having been developed only 10,000 years ago.

how long we've had language ———————————

how long we've had writing systems   ————————

how long we've had prescriptive grammars   —

The authors of prescriptive grammars are usually self-appointed authorities of language. The stereotype of the 18th-century grammarian is the clergyman, retired gentleman, or amateur philosopher,[31] persons for whom grammar is a hobby. Today there is no academic degree in prescriptive grammar. The closest degree is in linguistics but those who undertake study in this field, as it is currently defined, do not take a prescriptive approach when they engage in grammar-writing. Modern linguists, those trained since the mid-20th century, write descriptive grammars so as to document previously undescribed languages or in order to collect the facts about a language all in one place. The work produced can then be used both as a reference guide and for further research into the nature of language itself. The relationship between a prescriptive grammarian and a linguist is like the relationship between an etiquette expert and an anthropologist. One tells you how to act in a way that is considered "proper" in certain social situations while the other is engaged in a field of study, recognized by institutions of higher learning, that ultimately reveals something about the nature of being human.

The rise of prescriptive grammars has been traced to a time when good pronunciation and grammar became marketable assets—particularly for the socially aspiring middle class.[32] Linguistically insecure middle-class readers sought ways to distinguish themselves from the vulgar speech of their social inferiors and were therefore interested in manuals advising them on how to do so. By the first half of the 20th century the potential for profit-making had been discovered and the selling of "Good English" was taken over by entrepreneurs whose strongest skills were in the area of marketing rather than grammar.[33]

In practice, the experts in "good" grammar at any given time are those who are responsible for enforcing its use. They include schoolteachers, university professors, copy editors, and journalists who take it upon themselves to issue guidelines for their colleagues at media outlets. What they, and the grammars they consult, rely on are norms of use. If a critical mass of educated speakers adopt a new word or phrase, or cease to use a traditional one, the experts will incorporate this into their canon. This use-by-consensus aspect of language is most evident for new creations—the ones for which the rules have yet to be written. For instance, so far there is no formal grammar that includes the rule for how to use "lol" in electronic communication. For this reason, debates about the correct and incorrect uses of it spring up spontaneously on the Internet all the time. These debates are part of the process by which the conditions on its use evolve. Usage determines the rule, not the other way around. The terms of use of any innovative use of language is decided by the users and subsequently simply recorded rather than decreed by an authority figure.

There are authoritative works on how to use language (rather than simply describing it) that are not prescriptive. The in-house style guides used by publishing companies fall into this genre. They are clear on what the rules are and how they should be followed without any insinuation that their rules are the *only* ones, and the only ones that are good and correct. Indeed, their first concern is usually consistency. Ultimately the fallacy of authority derives from the notion that there is only one acceptable grammar for a given language—a notion that is unnecessarily restrictive and also untrue.

V

WHY DOES NON-STANDARD GRAMMAR PERSIST?

Given that there's an identifiable standard language, why doesn't everyone use it? It's certainly accessible. We hear it on television, read it in newspapers. It is taught in school and published in grammar books. So why does non-standard language persist?

The answer usually given is that people who are not using the standard language are lazy, stupid, and/or uneducated. They also tend not to be white, middle-class, and successful—an observation which may prompt us to ask if there are socioeconomic barriers to acquiring Standard English.

The story is much more complex and therefore much more interesting than that. The relationship between standard language and the middle class is not a matter of who has better access to the standard but, rather, whose dialect gets to constitute the standard in the first place. Given that there are numerous varieties of the same language being used at any given moment in time, the variety that is deemed "standard" depends to a large extent on who is using it. If people at the margins of society stop using *whom* it will still be part of Standard English. If the majority of the successful middle classes stop using *whom* it will, if it hasn't already, be declared dead.

The proliferation of many varieties of one dialect points to the constantly changing and fragmenting nature of language. What drives this process are a number of fundamental but not necessarily mutually compatible human needs. There is the need to innovate and be creative, the need on the part of the young to distinguish themselves from the old, the need to signal allegiance with others and to form collectives, etc. All of these drives are evident in fashion, as well. Fashion is clearly a choice, but so is style of speaking. People *choose* the way they speak.

In claiming that people choose the way they speak, we should be clear on what they are choosing. They are choosing to be creative, to style their language in a particular way, to mark their generation, and/or to sound like the people in the groups to which they want to belong—all of which are expanded on below. What they are not choosing are the connotations that their language may have, and indeed they may be unaware of these connotations. To take *ain't* as an example, if the people in my circles of friends, family, and acquaintances use *ain't*, I will too. To *not* use it may appear to be some sort of judgment on the language of those I love. By using *ain't*, however, I am not choosing to be considered an uneducated rural hick although I very well might be.

Examples of the unconventional as an expression of creativity abound. Consider the unconventional spelling of names—band names (*Limp Bizkit, Outkast, Noize*), product names (*Krispy Kreme* Doughnuts), and proper names (*Madisyn, Jessiqua, Zackerie, Joshuwa*). These alternative spellings are intended to grab attention or evoke a sense of uniqueness. Creativity overlaps with humour and playing with language can be an expression of both. On the Internet a popular phenomenon involves publicly posting the image of a cat with superimposed text, resulting in something called a lolcat. The caption on a lolcat always features poor grammar and egregious misspellings (e.g., "I are crying cuz I are out of focuss"). People go to some effort to craft these captions and there appear to be rules emerging for the "correct" use of LOLspeak[34].

There are aesthetic considerations in the use of non-standard language. Consider singing any of the following lyrics using standard *any* rather than non-standard *no*:

> *I can't get no satisfaction* — Rolling Stones
> *We don't need no education* — Pink Floyd
> *I don't want no scrub* — TLC

In these cases the choice of standard vs. non-standard also involves number of syllables. For song lyrics which are sung and set to music, the issue of one or two syllables matters. But of course there are cases where the choice of non-standard is not driven by rhyme and meter but simply to signal a kind of coolness as in Timbaland's *the way I are* or Rihanna singing *is you big enough* in *Rude boy.*

Each generation of young people invents their own set of slang terms. This happens with such regularity that given a set of terms (*airhead, bite me, wiggin'* vs. *random, emo, sweet*) one can accurately predict the decade of adolescence. Beyond vocabulary, the young also slightly alter their pronunciations, particularly vowels, from generation to generation as part of their process of differentiation. The vowel in *cool* is gradually coming to sound more like the vowel in *cute*, for instance, among adolescent and pre-adolescent Canadians. This gives kids their own accent, which is, predictably, perceived by older adults as an improper mastery of the language. Any investigator of language change in virtually any community has found the elders of the community to be of the opinion that the language is in decline, if not dying, based on the way it is used by the youngest generation.

One of the most vital functions of non-standard language is to create solidarity with others. It is a way of expressing non-conformity. Non-standard language can signal a stance taken towards authority and social norms. But crucially, like the standard, non-standard language is created with others, it is a collective effort, a shared code. No one can make up a non-standard dialect nor create slang on their own—the success of any form of language as a shared code depends on others picking it up and using it too. To use a fashion analogy once again, any daring fashion statement starts with just a few people but must be copied by the so-called early adopters[35] in order to become a bona fide trend.

In its function as a marker of solidarity, non-standard language can be shared among members of stigmatized and minority groups as one of their in-group signifiers. This complicates the issue of whose language is represented by the standard. On the one hand the language variety used by the powerful is more likely to be the standard, but on the other hand those excluded from power may actively resist using standard speech.

The resistance to the language of power shows up in adolescent and pre-adolescent speech long before categorization by class can be meaningfully applied.[36] Research has shown that the grammar of high school students, for example, right down to their vowels, varies systematically depending on whether they are institutionally or locally oriented. The users of the variety that is closer to the standard, the "jocks," participate in varsity sports, serve on student councils and are college-bound. Those who use non-standard varieties, e.g., the "burnouts," "freaks," "jells," etc.,[37] base their lives and activities outside of the school and are bound for the blue-collar workplace. These social categories mirror a fact about language in general— that standard speech is maintained and perpetuated by our national institutions: media, government, and school. As such, standard speech is associated with being urban and stands in contrast with the rural where we find the local vernacular, the slower-to-change and more specific-to-place dialects of those who reside outside major cities.

The solidarity-evoking function of a more local and casual vernacular was on display in the speech of Sarah Palin during her run as the vice-presidential nominee of the Republican Party in the 2008 U.S. presidential election. Her choice of words, syntax, and pronunciation were much commented on and parodied. Her speaking style was more casual (*you betcha*) and local than the classic neutral standard for political speech. As such it was in keeping with her positioning of herself as outside the centres of power and influence in both media and politics. Interestingly, however, she carried this out in the service of a conservative agenda which, as we will see in the next section, is at odds with the way the politics of standard vs. non-standard is ordinarily construed.

VI

WORDS AND THEIR CONNOTATIONS

When we consider the meaning of a word we usually first think of what it signifies in the world, that is we think of what it denotes. In the case of nouns, we think of the set of things in the world that they can pick out. For example, the noun *dog* denotes the set of things that have four legs, fur, bark, etc. In the case of verbs we think of the actions they name. The verb *climb* refers to ascending by use of the limbs. But in addition to their denotations, words also have a set of connotations. This is the domain of semiotics. So in addition to what part of the colour spectrum they pick out (what they denote), our colour terms also signify other things. Black is used for mourning, red is the colour of danger, green is associated with the environment, and so on. The popular catchphrase that has the form "X is the new Y" originated with colours and plays on their connotations. A statement like "brown is the new black" would be utterly nonsensical if we were thinking of denotation rather than connotation.

The terms *prescriptive* and *descriptive* also come with a set of connotations, especially when used in contrast with one another. When a linguist is consulted on how a word ought to be pronounced or spelled, for instance, the questioner is likely to hear about the distinction between prescriptive and descriptive approaches. The distinction is made in order to explain why a linguist will rarely, if ever, endorse a particular form over another. Often, this position gets construed as political. The descriptive approach is cast as once in which "anything goes" or, worse, as chaotic and anarchic. The prescriptive approach in contrast is seen as respectful of tradition and the upholding of societal standards. In this way prescriptivists play the role of language conservatives while descriptive grammarians are considered language liberals.

The connection between prescriptivism and the maintenance of respect and values is made explicit by Robert Hartwell Fiske (to take just one example), editor and publisher of the online magazine *The Vocabula Review*, the slogan for which used to read "A society is generally as lax as its language." On the "About TVR" page[38] we find the familiar claims about English undergoing devolution:

> Along with the evolution of language—the thousands of neologisms that new technologies and new thinking

have brought about, for instance—there has been a concurrent, if perhaps less recognizable, devolution of language. The English language has become more precise for some users of it while becoming more plodding for others. Not a small part of this new cumbrousness is due to the loss of distinctions between words, the misuse of words, and other abuses of language.

What is missing is any identification of the people to whom English is becoming less clear and precise. Why would Standard English be *more* clear to someone who speaks non-standard English than their own dialect would be? Clarity can only be assessed by the person to whom a message is addressed; it does not lie in the message itself.

The political metaphor for the prescriptive/descriptive opposition is simply that, a metaphor.[39] The superimposing of the right vs. left metaphor onto positions on language is nonsensical at its core. Nor is there any coherence to associating political positions with dialects themselves. Users of local dialects in rural settings tend to be social conservatives. Does this mean Standard English is the language of the left? For their part, linguists who are committed to a descriptive view of languages and dialects often consider prescriptivists to be unenlightened people who have not embraced science as a means of understanding complex phenomena. This plays on another metaphor (science as rational) that is perhaps equally open to debate.

Descriptive grammarians and linguists require training to do what they do. The study of linguistics is a scholarly pursuit that takes many years and, perhaps because of that, is undertaken by a small number of people. People with prescriptive views on language express their positions through various means: letters to the editor, Facebook groups, blogs, etc. They form societies and support groups and engage in forms of public protest against what they see as the lax and declining standards of speech. Since public protest is tied to minority positions, this gives the illusion that prescriptivists are in the minority. In fact, these defenders of standards, tradition, and values when it comes to language vastly outnumber the scholars of linguistics.

What is lost when we engage in these sorts of characterizations are questions of substance such as what is the best way of teaching Standard English to speakers of non-standard dialects. Is it more effective to tell someone using *ain't* that they are careless and contributing to the degradation of the English language or to tell them that the use of this word in a job interview might jeopardize their chances of getting the job? Which serves as the greater motivator for the acquisition of Standard English?

VII

IN DEFENCE OF A STANDARD

Arguments against prescriptivism are not to be conflated with arguments against having a standard, or common, form of a given language. The arguments against prescriptivism are arguments against considering one form of language to be inherently better than another. It is good to have a standard, but the standard is not "good."

A standard form of a language serves as a lingua franca among people who speak different dialects of that language. It is simply a common language. Having one shared form of language is a way to transcend local differences. We need one common representative form that can be taught both to the young and to speakers of other languages. We need one common representative form that can be used in official documents, print media, and on our national airwaves. To borrow an argument from the English-only movement in the United States, it is cost-effective to have one standard language. It is important that this dialect be actively maintained. It must be updated to keep up with the changes the language undergoes but must be free of jargon and slang which are particular to certain groups and not shared by all.

The arguments for a standard writing system are even more compelling. A stable writing system can allow us to read and understand what people wrote long ago without the need for translation. It provides a common means of communication among people with different accents and sometimes among people who speak different languages (e.g., Mandarin and Cantonese speakers do not understand each other but can both read written Chinese). It is helpful to have different spellings for homophones (e.g., *to/too/two*) so as to reduce ambiguity in written texts.

It is possible to make arguments for one form of language to serve as our common one without elevating it (and the users of it) to some higher moral status. Perhaps the most tragic consequence of a prescriptive view that there is only one acceptable way of speaking is that we are unable to recognize anything *other* than the approved variety. When we hear non-standard dialects, we don't hear difference and diversity but only a degraded form of standard speech. The promulgation of a standard above and instead of all else is like arguing that people should all wear a uniform, or that all small towns should have the same stores: Walmart, McDonald's, and Starbucks. We don't need this level of standardization.

Arguing that it is good to have a standard language variety but that that variety should not be imbued with evaluative appraisals like "correct" or "better" may seem like a paradox. It is not if we recognize that humans are more than capable of mastering more than one dialect and more than one writing system. Indeed, humans are capable of mastering more than one *language*. Multilingualism has been the norm, not the exception, throughout history in most of the world.[40] Recognizing and celebrating a non-standard dialect is of no threat to the existence of a standard if speakers know and use both appropriately. The existence of a streamlined and more efficient writing system (e.g., text-messaging conventions like *u* for *you*, *4* for *for*, etc.) is of no threat to our standard spelling system if people can use both and know when to do so. Our schools should be the site of learning about standard speaking, reading, writing, and spelling but these should be taught as additions to the systems their students already know, not as replacements. After all, most young people have learned text-speak and punctuation conventions on Twitter and Facebook on their own time *despite* what they are being taught in school. This speaks to our extraordinary capacity to learn new conventions quickly. These learning capabilities can more than accommodate the mastery of numerous styles of language.

VIII

WHY DOES GRAMMAR MATTER?

When an individual airs their pet peeve about people who say *anyways* or who write *your* when they should be writing *you're*, when they shudder at a non-standard dialect or send off a note to their newspaper about a grammatical error found in a news article, they may be expressing nothing more than irritation and concern. But given the number of people who share the same concerns and who express them over time and across cultures, it is likely that there are deeper issues involved.

To start with the obvious, grammar matters because tradition matters. We carry on traditions in many realms of our lives. Insisting on maintaining the distinction between *your* and *you're* is a nod to the way we have written these words over time. Like the QWERTY keyboard, the traditional way may not be the most logical or efficient but it has status simply as the system that has endured.

An insistence on there being a "right" and "wrong" way to use language serves to justify the way we have been taught. It is a way of demonstrating lessons learned and presenting oneself as the product of a good education. Correcting someone else's grammar may be a way of asserting superiority, judgment, and power over them, not just their language use.

The concern over the way others use language may also stem from a sense of tribalism, a my-group-is-better-than-your-group orientation. Just as a particular dialect evolves among speakers in contact, the disdain for that dialect unites the people outside that group. Solidarity can be created by a shared loathing of how "other" people talk. Language as a means of distinguishing social groups is hypothesized to reach back into prehistoric times and is offered as an explanation for why children appear to be more sensitive to accent than race when choosing friends.[41] In a milder form, connections among people can be formed on the basis of shared humour when mimicking certain speech styles (e.g., postmodern, academic, bureaucratic, etc.).

In some cases, outrage over the way people speak may represent confusion of style with substance. The true offence may be how little some people have to say in their expletive-laden rants or their poorly spelled messages. The appreciation of good grammar may really be an appreciation of eloquence and insight. Eloquence and insight, however, do not come in only one style. The eloquence of Harlem street kids playing The Dozens or the insight of a community elder who uses the local dialect can be assessed independently of the style of language used.

Another theme running through prescriptive views is the fear and distrust associated with change and the idea that change leads to loss. Language change is equated with language decline and change is never viewed as being for the better. Bemoaning the state of the language among "the kids these days" usually involves cataloguing what they don't do anymore rather than careful consideration of what they do that is new. This collective anxiety around change extends far beyond language into other realms: television will kill radio, video will kill film, etc. Dennis Baron, writing about our complicated relationship to computers in his book *A Better Pencil*,[42] points out that virtually all writing implements have been greeted with anxiety and outrage at when they were first introduced. For example, typewriters were predicted to destroy the art of handwriting. As for writing itself, there are oral cultures today the members of which believe that the development of a writing system will irrevocably change the language for the worse.

CONCLUSION

In asking the question why people are more likely to have a pet peeve about language than they are about other burdens of modern capitalism (illogical grocery store layouts, interminable automated phone messages that have replaced operators, etc.), what is immediately clear is that there is a genuine interest in language and the way it is used. People feel invested in their own use of language and therefore in the way it is similar to and different from others'. This interest need not be expressed in terms of prejudice. The knowledge that all humans are capable of expressing themselves in a variety of ways means that we need only agree on which styles of language are appropriate for which contexts. Saying one style is better suited to a specific context than another does not mean it is *inherently* better, however.

The articulating of judgments about language may be part of the very function of language itself. While it is commonly held that the purpose of language is communication, there are theories about its evolution that suggest that, like singing, it arose as a means of externalizing thought.[43] Complaining may have more in common with clapping, cheering, gasping, screaming, and swearing than with reason and argument as a way of communicating nothing more than a reaction.

If we shift our way of thinking about language away from prescriptivist views, we may liberate ourselves in the process. Grammar not only plays a role in the way language is *used*, known as language production. It also plays a role in how we *understand* language as well, i.e., language comprehension. Almost everyone has had the painful experience of knowing that their comprehension is only partial—situations like writing tests, signing legal contracts, or following assembly instructions. Prescriptive notions of "correct" language and the "laziness" of people who don't use it can evoke feelings of insecurity or embarrassment that prevent us from acknowledging our difficulty with an unfamiliar style of language and seeking a translation. The clarity that prescriptivists seek to preserve in language is in fact something that must be constantly negotiated as language shifts and turns. We must engage in these debates about language confidently rather than with a sense of shame. Ultimately, letting go of prescriptivism will permit us to truly enjoy a far greater range of expression than the narrow channel we think of as "correct."

ACKNOWLEDGMENTS

I would like to thank Peter Ives, who has been involved with this book at every step of the way and who has provided much enthusiastic encouragement, valuable help, and stimulating input. Although this is a short book, I would still like to make a full-length dedication to three linguists who inspire me, though there are many more. Deborah Cameron, Penny Eckert, and Geoff Pullum have each deeply influenced my thinking about language and all three have written about the same issues with far more eloquence and depth than I have done here. I hope anyone who is interested in language reads some of their work.

ENDNOTES

1   Stephen Fry's essay entitled "Don't mind your lan-
    guage" was posted on his blog November 4, 2008, and
    can be found at <www.stephenfry.com/2008/11/04/
    dont-mind-your-language%E2%80%A6/>.

2   See Jila Ghomeshi, Ray Jackendoff, Nicole Rosen & Kevin Russell
    "Contrastive focus reduplication in English (the salad-salad paper),"
    Natural Language & Linguistic Theory, 22, 2004, pp. 307–357. For
    a corpus of examples see <home.cc.umanitoba.ca/~krussll/
    redup-corpus.html>.

3   Lists of years gone by can be found at <www.lssu.edu/banished/>.

4   See <languagelog.ldc.upenn.edu/nll/>.

5   Geoff Nunberg, *Going Nucular* (New York: Public Affairs, 2004).
    See also his website "Fresh Air" commentary, October 2, 2002,
    <people.ischool.berkeley.edu/~nunberg/nucular.html>.

6   See this page on the linguist Jack Chambers' website for other
    examples and discussion: <www.chass.utoronto.ca/~chambers/
    changes.html>.

7   The trilled "r" was the subject of a radio piece on *C'est la vie*, CBC Radio One, April 5 and 7, 2009 in which a francophone talked about being aware that he used the "wrong 'r'" and about the shame and embarrassment that engendered.

8   The faculty of the Department of Linguistics at the University of Arizona responded with a statement that was sent to the governor of Arizona and the superintendent of public instruction. It can be found here: <www.u.arizona.edu/~hammond/ling_state-ment_final.pdf> See also the following piece from the *Arizona Daily Star* published on July 13, 2010, and written by linguists: <azstarnet.com/news/opinion/article_bfb4230b-43b0-5e92-975a-580456386279.html>. The Linguistic Society of America issued a resolution that spoke out against the Arizona Teachers' English Fluency Initiative in mid-August 2010. It can be found here: <www.lsadc.org/info/lsa-res-arizona.cfm>.

9   See <www.apostrophe.org.uk/>.

10 We also use pronouns like *it, this, that* to refer to things but I'll leave those aside.

11 Epicene means gender-neutral in this context.

12 For a discussion of the history of singular *they* and the proscriptions against it, see Ann Bodine, "Androcentrism in prescriptive grammar: singular 'they,' sex-indefinite 'he,' and 'he or she,' *Language in Society* 4, 1975, pp.129–46. See also Henry Churchyard's website for numerous entertaining examples, discussion, and more references: <www.crossmyt.com/hc/linghebr/austheir.html>.

13 Rodney D. Huddleston and Geoffrey K. Pullum, *A Student's Introduction to English Grammar* (Cambridge: Cambridge University Press, 2005), p.16.

14 A more comprehensive and entertaining summary of the history of this term is provided by Deborah Cameron in her book *Verbal Hygiene* (London: Routledge, 1995, pp. 123–7).

15 "Queer" meaning "homosexual" is often cited as a reclaimed word but has gone on to cover much more territory as an umbrella term for non-heterosexual sexuality, for identity, community, and, within academia, as the name for a theoretical framework.

16 This term was introduced by the French deconstructionist Roland Barthes and taken up by media scholar John Fiske. See Robin Lakoff's *The Language War* (Berkeley: University of California Press, 2000), pp. 53–4 for discussion with regard to language and linguistics. The term refers to the process by which a majority (i.e., in-power) group loses defining characteristics and is perceived as universal and/or natural.

17 Eckert & McConnell-Ginet introduce this term to talk about why white people don't have a "race" and heterosexuals don't have a "lifestyle." See Penelope Eckert and Sally McConnell-Ginet *Language and Gender* (Cambridge: Cambridge University Press, 2003).

18 See Rebecca Traister's article in *Salon* magazine <www.salon.com/life/broadsheet/2010/06/01/palin_feminism/> on Sarah Palin's grab for feminism and Traister's call to the Left to fight for the word.

19 The use of "apartheid" in reference to Israel has provoked a fractious debate among the members of the Pride community in Toronto. See <www.pridetoronto.com/press/pride-toronto-disallows-phrase-israeli-apartheid-in-2010-parade/> about the decision to ban a group using this term which was subsequently reversed.

20 The saying is attributed to Max Weinreich, a Yiddish linguist, from about 1945, but not without some debate.

21 For the official LSA response see <www.lsadc.org/info/lsa-res-ebonics.cfm>. See also this link <www.cal.org/topics/dialects/tesolebo.html> for the statement by the association of the Teachers of English to Speakers of Other Languages (TESOL).

22 See <open.salon.com/content.php?cid=89619>, see also <www.nytimes.com/2009/01/11/us/11english. html?_r=2&scp=1&sq=english%20only&st=cse>.

23 I am leaving aside the strong genitive pronouns: *mine, ours, yours, his, hers, theirs.* These pronouns appear on their own without a following possessor so that we get the following contrast: *that is my book* vs. *that book is mine.*

24 The facts in this paragraph come from Victoria Fromkin, Robert Rodman, Nina Hyams and Kirsten M. Hummel, *An Introduction to Language*, 3rd Canadian ed. (Toronto: Nelson, 2006).

25 Polysemy can be contrasted with homonymy where a word has different and *un*related meanings. The word *bank* meaning the raised edge of a river vs. a financial institution is homonymous.

26 The examples and discussion of them is taken from John R. Taylor, *Linguistic Categorization*, 3rd ed., (Oxford: Oxford University Press, 2003).

27 All examples of metaphor are taken from George Lakoff and Mark Johnson's influential work *Metaphors We Live By*, (Chicago: University of Chicago Press, 1980).

28 These examples are from John R. Taylor, *Linguistic Categorization*, 3rd ed. (Oxford: Oxford University Press, 2003).

29 See <timberens.com/interviews/alden.htm>.

30 David Crystal, *How Language Works* (New York: The Overlook Press, 2006), p. 356.

31 See Joan Beal and Massimo Sturiale's introduction to the following book for discussion of research that calls the stereotype into question. Joan C. Beal, Carmela Nocera, and Massimo Sturiale (eds.), *Perspectives on Prescriptivism*, (Peter Lang: Bern, Germany, 2008), p. 10.

32 See Joan C. Beal's "Shamed by your English?": the Market Value of a "Good" Pronunciation in Joan C. Beal, Carmela Nocera, and Massimo Sturiale (eds.), *Perspectives on Prescriptivism*, (Peter Lang: Bern, Germany, 2008) pp. 21–40.

33 See the entertaining book by Edwin L. Battistella, *Do you make these mistakes in English? The story of Sherwin Cody's Famous Language School* (Oxford: Oxford University Press, 2008).

34 See <speaklolspeak.com/page/LOLspeak+101>.

35 For a description of the full cast of characters involved in the spreading of a fashion "epidemic" see Malcolm Gladwell, *The Tipping Point* (New York: Back Bay Books/Little, Brown and Company, 2000).

36 Penny Eckert has studied the dialects of American adolescents and pre-adolescents precisely because she is interested in what might be playing a role in the way they style their speech before traditional class distinctions (based as on labour) apply. See, for instance, Penelope Eckert, *Linguistic Variation as Social Practice: The Linguistic Construction of Social Meaning in Belten High* (Oxford: Blackwell, 2000).

37 Names for this social category vary with time and place while, interestingly, "jock" remains relatively constant. This is connected to the fact that the name for any normative category (straight, white, able-bodied) undergoes few changes, if it is used as all. Within the North American educational system, "jock" is a normative category.

38 See <www.vocabula.com/VRabout.asp>.

39 This metaphor is used to great effect in David Foster Wallace's article "Tense Present: Democracy, English, and the Wars over Usage" published in *Harper's Magazine* in April 2001.

40 See the statement to this effect on the website of the *Linguistic Society of America* <www.lsadc.org/info/ling-fields-multi.cfm>. Further references are given there.

41 See Katherine D. Kinzler, Kristin Shutts, Jasmine DeJesus, Elizabeth S. Spelke (2009) "Accent Trumps Race in Guiding Children's Social Preferences," *Social Cognition,* Vol. 27:4, pp. 623–634.

42 Dennis Baron, *A Better Pencil: Readers, Writers, and the Digital Revolution* (Oxford: Oxford University Press, 2009).

43 See Steven J. Mithen, *The Singing Neanderthals: the origins of music, language, mind and body* (London: Weidenfeld & Nicolson Ltd., 2005).